IT'S TRUE!

Animals Are
Electrifying

IT'S TRUE! You can collect the whole set
IT'S TRUE! You'll be surprised and amazed
IT'S TRUE! These books are the best,
full of fantastic trivia, gory details
and incredible stories

*Titles already published on* HAIR, CRIME,
BUGS, FROGS, ROMANS, FLIGHT, DINOSAURS,
LIFE BEFORE DINOSAURS, BUSHFIRES, FASHION,
ANIMALS, EXPLORERS

*Titles coming up on* RUBBISH, THE SUPERNATURAL,
SPACE, EVEREST, SPIES, ANTARCTICA, BUSHRANGERS,
SQUID, BONES, and more

find out all about it on
www.itstrue.com.au

Rick Wilkinson

PICTURES BY Mic Looby

# IT'S TRUE!

# Animals Are Electrifying

ALLEN&UNWIN

First published in 2005

Allen & Unwin
83 Alexander Street
Crows Nest NSW 2065
Australia
Phone: (61 2) 8425 0100
Fax: (61 2) 9906 2218
Email: info@allenandunwin.com
Web: www.allenandunwin.com

National Library of Australia
Cataloguing-in-Publication entry:

Wilkinson, Rick, 1947– .
It's true! animals are electrifying.
Includes index.
For children.
ISBN 1 74114 343 8.
1. Animals – Juvenile literature. I. Looby, Mic. II. Title.
590

Series, cover and text design by Ruth Grüner
Cover photographs: large puffer, Stuart Westmoreland/Getty Images
small puffer, Steven Hunt/Getty Images
Set in 12.5pt Minion by Ruth Grüner
Printed by McPherson's Printing Group

1 3 5 7 9 10 8 6 4 2

**Teaching notes for the It's True! series are available
on the website: www.itstrue.com.au**

# CONTENTS

**WHY ANIMALS?**

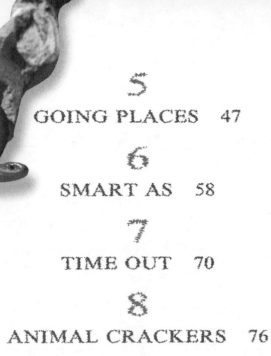

# Why animals?

Some of my first playmates were animals. Well, insects really. I found them living under our lemon tree. They looked like leaves, or sticks, or bits of bark, and I wondered why. Was it a disguise so they could steal lemons when no one was looking?

Later on I saw lots more wild animals, large and small, in the Australian bush and in places like Africa, Papua New Guinea and Canada. I still had questions. How could some live in both water and air? How could others see in the dark? Did some creatures really go without food all winter?

The animals couldn't tell me, so I pestered the scientists who study them. I soon discovered stories of incredible abilities, amazing escapes and gruesome death in the fight for survival – stranger than any video game. They happen all around us every day.

Rick Wilkinson

# 1

# DEADLY

Have you heard that some birds drink blood, tarantulas throw darts, stoats are hypnotists and rabbits eat their own poo (yuk!)? Why do they do those things?

Life in the wild is a continuing fight for survival. All living things – animals and plants, both large and small – need food to stay alive. But there is a lot of competition out there, so to survive, each species has come up with a way of obtaining food that is different from all the others.

Some animal species, like the ones in this chapter, have developed amazing and very effective ways of catching their prey.

# Zapped

All animals, including humans, have electricity in their bodies. Electric currents flow in living tissues such as nerves and muscles, taking signals to and from the brain. Some animals are also able to generate electricity that goes outside their bodies. Several species of stingrays and catfish stun their prey (small fish, crabs, shrimps, even small mammals that venture into the water) with electrical discharges. These fish have organs in their bodies (usually in the tail) that act like a battery. The 'batteries' are made up of thousands of compact nerve endings controlled by the fish's brain. That means the fish can turn on its weapon any time it wants. It is very effective in water because water is a good conductor of electricity. With rays and catfish, the first discharge is the strongest, and often the fish has to rest after making several zaps in a short time.

The larger the fish, the stronger the charge. For instance, a full-grown 20-kilogram electric catfish found in West Africa can discharge up to 450 volts. Local fishermen have learnt to handle them with care. But the real shocker is an electric eel found in rivers in South America. It can discharge 500 volts, sometimes more. That's enough to light up your whole house!

Why don't electric fish and eels electrocute themselves? We're not sure. Perhaps something in the skin and the nerve tissues prevents a short-circuit.

## Detection device

Some other animals, like the platypus and the echidna in Australia, use electricity to find food. They have fine-tuned sensors that can pick up an electrical charge made by their prey and guide them to their meal.

For instance, freshwater shrimps, worms and termites generate tiny electrical charges as they move about – sometimes as low as 500 millionths (0.0005) of a volt. You and I wouldn't have a hope of feeling that tiny shock, even if we had our hands right on top of it. But the platypus and the echidna can, even when the prey is buried in a river bed or in a termite nest below ground.

When a platypus dives, flaps of skin seal tightly over its ears and eyes, so that it is blind and deaf when it swims underwater. It homes in on shrimps and worms using an electronic sensor in its soft leathery bill, waving this from side to side as it swims to scan the river bed ahead. The echidna, which is a distant relative of the platypus, has a sensor on the end of its long snout. As it shuffles along, it can detect the faint movement of ants and termites under its feet. Once it finds a nest, the echidna quickly digs into its meal.

## SEA-BED SCANNER

The Pacific Spookfish lives more than
1000 metres down in the ocean. It has a long,
thin snout with mucus-filled sensors on the
underside. The fish uses this snout to scan for
electric charges made by crabs and shellfish
buried in the sea bed (a bit like a beachcomber
sweeping across the sand with a metal
detector, looking for lost coins and rings).

## Super Smell

One of the most efficient ocean hunters in the sea is the
shark. Not only can its sensors pick up the vibrations
of a struggling fish about 1½ kilometres away, it can
smell a single drop of blood in the water more than
half a kilometre off.

Another ferocious predator is the polar bear.
Some people say it's more dangerous to humans than
a grizzly bear. It has a super-keen sense of smell, so
you'd better not keep smelly food in your tent at night

when camping in polar bear territory. The animal can home in on a dead whale or walrus from 30 kilometres away. Normally, though, polar bears catch live prey, especially seals. They sniff out holes in the Arctic ice where seals come up to breathe. They can do that from a long way off even if a seal hasn't been there for a while and the hole is covered in snow a metre thick.

A bear will wait by the hole till a seal pops up for air. Then it pounces, smashing the seal's skull.

## Mugger

The animal world has its share of thugs too. Take the frigate bird that lives around Australian coasts and in the Pacific islands. It doesn't have webbed feet and its feathers are not waterproof, so it can't swim. But it has a huge wingspan of about 2 metres and is an amazing acrobat in flight. It can skim low over the sea and snatch fish near the surface with its hooked beak.

Another way to get food is to mug and rob other birds. The frigate bird can tell when another seabird is flying home with a catch. It will swoop down and attack the other bird in mid-flight, forcing the victim to drop or disgorge its fish. The frigate bird instantly goes into a dive, catches the fish before it hits the water and makes off with it.

Frigate birds are kidnappers as well as robbers. They will snatch young seabirds from unprotected nests and kill them while their parents are away.

# Bolt from the blue

Another lethal speedster is the Peregrine Falcon. It's the fastest bird in the world, reaching speeds of over 300 kilometres per hour. The Peregrine Falcon uses this speed to prey on other birds in flight. It hovers high in the sky and then comes hurtling down in a spectacular dive like an attacking fighter plane. The other bird is killed by the force of the impact, while the faster-moving falcon is able to come out of its dive unhurt with the victim in its talons.

## Knockout

Small creatures can also pack a punch. There's a tough little guy called a mantis shrimp that lives in shallow tropical and sub-tropical seas. It has an extension of its main claw that's kept folded out of sight, a bit like the sheathed blade of a pocket-knife. To overpower prey, the shrimp flicks open its claw extension at unbelievable speed and smashes into the victim. It's one of the fastest actions known for any animal. A large Californian mantis shrimp (which is about 25 centimetres long) can have a strike speed of 10 metres per second. That's about the speed of a bullet fired from a .22 calibre rifle. It cuts a small fish in two and cracks open the shells of crabs and shellfish to get at the flesh inside. It can also split open the finger of an unlucky fisherman.

Aquarium managers are very wary of these shrimps because they have been known to crack the side of a double-walled, safety-glass fish tank with their 'flick-knife'. That leaves a lot of mopping up, not to mention buying a new tank and maybe new fish.

## Casting a Spell

The stoat, a small furry creature with a long, slim body like a ferret, has a gentler way to catch its meal – often a bird or a rabbit. It casts a sort of magic spell.

I don't mean it pulls the bird or rabbit out of a hat.
The stoat doesn't have a hat, but it could go on the
stage as a hypnotist. It performs a weird, swaying dance
to mesmerise its prey. Really it's a dance of death.
The watching bird or rabbit goes into a trance and
won't try to get away as the stoat slowly dances closer
and closer. Suddenly the stoat will lunge and kill with
a swift bite to the neck before the victim has time to
snap out of its daze and escape.

# Submariner

One of the most amazing specialists must be the spider
that hunts for its prey underwater using a diving bell
or capsule. The spider makes the capsule by weaving
a tight web and attaching it to a plant stem below the
water surface. Then it captures air bubbles in the hairs
on its stomach to take down and release under the web.
Gradually, like blowing up a balloon, the web fills out
to make a trapped air pocket that is large enough for
the spider to live in. From this underwater home,
it dives out to surprise and catch passing tadpoles,

small fish and other pond creatures that
it could not reach from the surface.
They would hardly expect to see
a spider suddenly appear in their
midst without an aqualung tank
and face mask.

To provide the oxygen it needs to
stay alive, the diving spider goes to the surface every
now and then, captures more air bubbles and brings
them down to the web. It's not just a hunting lodge,
either. The spider eats, mates and brings up its young
in the underwater chamber.

## Blood for dinner

To end this chapter on a bloody note, let's talk about
vampire bats. All the horror stories, like Count
Dracula, come from three types of bats in central and
South America. They must drink blood, which is rich
in nutrients, to stay alive. Two of these bats only drink
the blood of birds. The third feeds mostly on mammals
like cattle and horses, but sometimes also on humans.

This bat comes silently in the night and uses a heat-sensor in its nose to locate blood vessels close to the surface, perhaps in an ear lobe or a toe that's sticking out of the bedclothes. It doesn't leave puncture marks as in the vampire movies, and its front teeth are so razor-sharp that you can't even feel the bite. The bat cuts out a small sliver of flesh without waking the victim. Its saliva has a chemical that keeps the blood from clotting as it laps up its fill.

Vampire bats don't take much, maybe 30 millilitres (about two teaspoons) each, but the anti-clotting chemical keeps working after they've gone, so a small baby could bleed to death. If you were bitten, would you hide under the covers next night to make sure it didn't happen again? I know I would.

But horses and cattle can't escape, so the bats will return to the same victim each night. After a few days, the animal is so weak it can hardly stand.

It's not just the bats that are 'bloodthirsty'. There's a small bird in the Galapagos Islands that has been nicknamed a vampire finch. It's very dry for most of the year in this bird's island home, and plant seeds produced after brief periods of rain are quickly eaten. So the vampire finch turns to large seabirds like the booby to help it survive the long periods of drought. Sometimes the finch will smash a booby's egg by rolling it off a ledge to get at the yolk. But more often it will drink the booby's blood to get the nutrients it needs. The finch pecks away at the booby's tail feathers, breaking off some of the quills and causing blood to flow.

You'd think the booby would get a bit upset at being jabbed in the backside, and do something about it. Maybe it just doesn't feel any pain. Anyway, check out the next chapter and you'll find some creatures that do have spectacular and unusual ways of fighting back.

# 2
# FIGHTING BACK

In the fight for survival, all living organisms have developed ways of defending themselves and protecting their young. Sometimes the young have defences of their own. Many animals, even small ones, are ferocious fighters and have ingenious weapons. Others use cunning and less aggressive tactics against attackers.

# The incredible fart

You have probably heard of snakes that
hiss or rattle their tails to warn off predators.
Well, there are two types of snake found
in North America that prefer to fart
at their enemies instead. Both have
odd names – the Sonoran Coral Snake and
the Western Hook-nosed Snake – and they
are fairly small. But the farts, which polite scientists call
'cloacal popping', meaning the sound coming from the
reptile's excretion sac, are loud enough to be heard
up to 2 metres away. The snakes can fire off a few in
quick succession and they sound very like human
farts. It must be a handy excuse for
bushwalkers in the area who've
eaten baked beans for breakfast.

## Bums away!

There's a small black and yellow beetle, called a
Bombardier Beetle, found in most parts of the world

15

that can shoot a scalding hot chemical spray out of its backside. It's called a Bombardier Beetle because it can fire off 20 or 30 rounds in quick succession, *popopopopopopopop*! The mixture is strong enough to stun other insects and send bigger predators, like frogs, hopping away gasping for clean air.

# High-velocity vomit

Even more gross is the defence of the fulmar, a seabird found in cool-to-cold parts of the world. These birds defend their nests by making coughing noises and lunging at intruders, such as otters and other birds like skuas, ospreys and sea eagles. They also spew out jets of foul-smelling stomach oil. It's the only way young chicks can defend themselves when their parents are away foraging at sea for up to 20 hours at a time.

From their first moments out of the egg, hatchlings

oops...
sorry

have the ability
to vomit oil,
and their aim is very
good. At four days old
they can spew nearly half
a metre, while older chicks have a range of about
1½ metres. Apart from its bad smell, the stomach oil
clogs up feathers or hair. A predator
covered in the oil can become
waterlogged and drown.

## Blow Up

There's a fish called a pufferfish that blows up when
danger approaches. You may have seen one washed
up on the beach. They have round, plump bodies and
live mostly in warm coastal waters, eating shellfish,
crabs and sea urchins which they grind up in their
strong teeth.

When a predator like a shark or a dolphin, comes
near, pufferfish quickly suck water (or air if they're
out of the water) in through their gills to a sac inside.

Then they'll swell up into a round balloon-shape three times their normal size. Little spines hidden in their skin suddenly pop up so they look like prickly balls that don't seem so good to eat after all, like the ones on the cover of this book. When the danger passes, they expel the water and air out through their gills to return to normal size.

The pufferfish can swell up like this because it doesn't have any ribs or pelvic bones. Strong muscles in its thick, stretchable skin control its size and stop it bursting. Most pufferfish are quite small, about 15 centimetres long, but some species can measure 1 metre. They blow up into huge spiny beach balls when danger looms.

It doesn't always work, because sharks and some sharp-beaked wading birds, like herons, puncture the skin. But even in death the pufferfish can give a nasty surprise. Its organs contain a powerful poison that can kill a predator. In Japan, chefs have to be specially trained to cook pufferfish. Part of the exam is for the trainee chefs to eat the meal they prepare! You need to choose a restaurant carefully if that fish is on the menu.

# Slimebag

Now here's a real slippery customer that lives in cold waters up to 10 000 metres deep. It's a long (up to 80 centimetres) eel-like seafloor-dweller called a hagfish that has no scales, no bones and no jaws, just a gaping mouth and raspy tongue. Because it can produce bucket-loads of gooey muck when in trouble, it is also known as a slime eel. The slime is produced in glands along both sides of the creature's body. It comes out of the fish in concentrated form and then swells up when it seeps into the water. The goop is reinforced with tiny fibres that make it strong and difficult for an attacking fish to pull off. The result is a cocoon of slime that completely covers and protects the hagfish. That makes it a real slimebag.

The slime can suffocate an attacker by clogging its gills, but the hagfish itself 'sneezes' out any slime that gets in its own nostrils. When danger passes, it ties itself into a knot and then pushes the knot down its body to wipe the slime away.

# Playing possum

Have you ever pretended to be asleep when someone comes into your room so you won't be disturbed? It's called 'playing possum'. There's a marsupial in North America called an opossum that goes even further. It suddenly 'drops dead' when danger threatens.

This white-faced relative of the Australian possum doesn't have any strong defences against predators. It spends the day in a hollow tree, rock cavity or old burrow and comes out at night to feed on whatever it can find – insects, frogs, birds, eggs, berries, acorns and mushrooms. When attacked by a night raider like a fox or an owl, the opossum will open its mouth wide and snarl to scare the attacker away. If that doesn't work, it suddenly drools and blows bubbles of saliva out its nose, trying to look diseased and not good to eat.

As a last resort, the opossum flops over on its side and plays dead. It's very convincing. It hangs its tongue out and releases from its bottom green slime that smells like decayed flesh. Many predators get the urge to eat only after killing live prey, so they leave the 'dead' opossum alone. The opossum can play dead for up to six hours, but as soon as the danger has passed, it jumps up and runs off to continue its own hunt for a meal.

# Squirting blood

The horned lizard, which lives in the deserts of the USA and Mexico, has several ways of defending itself against predators like snakes, larger lizards and hawks. First it stays very still so that its dirt colours blend into the surroundings and make the lizard hard to see. If this doesn't work, it tries hissing and puffing up to look bigger and more menacing, showing the spikes on its body that give the reptile its name. If that fails, it has one last chance. The lizard shoots blood out of its eyes.

How does it do this? By increasing the blood pressure in its head and sinuses (pinch your nostrils shut and then try to blow your nose – gently – to get an idea of how it works). This ruptures tiny blood vessels and blood squirts out through the lizard's tear ducts. It's a gruesome sight. The lizard can fire a jet of blood and hit an attacker up to a metre away. The lizard's blood contains irritants, so a direct hit in an attacker's face will sting. Even if the blood doesn't hit, the squirting eye takes the predator by surprise and gives the lizard time to escape.

## Stinging Swinger

There are a few crab species living on tropical coral reefs that have been smart enough to use a bodyguard as a defence against predators. Some hermit crabs, for instance, find a sea anemone which they attach to the back of their shell home. The anemone's stinging tentacles are a sure way of keeping predators away. Scientists aren't sure what the anemone gets out of this, but maybe it gets 'paid' for its protection services by being transported around the coral reef area to places where food is plentiful.

The little boxer crab has taken this even further. It carries a small anemone in each of its two front pincers and uses them like a fistful of nettles. When threatened, the crab thrusts its pincers forward and the attacker (it might be a fish or an eel) is suddenly confronted by two bunches of stinging tentacles. The crab never lets go of the captive anemones while it's alive. This means it can't use its pincers to gather up and pass food to its mouth the way most crabs do. Boxer crabs use two front legs instead.

# Prickly customer

Other animals are fitted with their own detachable missiles. Some types of tarantula spiders have prickly, harpoon-like hairs on their abdomens which they flick at any attacker, using their back legs. These hairs have a barbed end that stings and causes an allergic reaction. Spider collectors handle tarantulas carefully because the hairs work their way into the skin and can cause a severe rash. But the little darts can do much more harm to a predator, like a bird or rodent, especially if the darts hit the eyes or mucus membranes. They can cause severe swelling in the throat and temporary or permanent blindness.

If you think some of these defence methods are gruesome, just wait till you read the next chapter and see how creatures of the same species treat each other.

# SKIN POISON

The deadliest defence of all is a toxin secreted through the skin of South American poison arrow frogs. They are the most poisonous animals in the world. One frog carries about 200 micrograms (200 millionths of a gram/0.0002 grams) of poison, and that's enough to kill 100 humans.

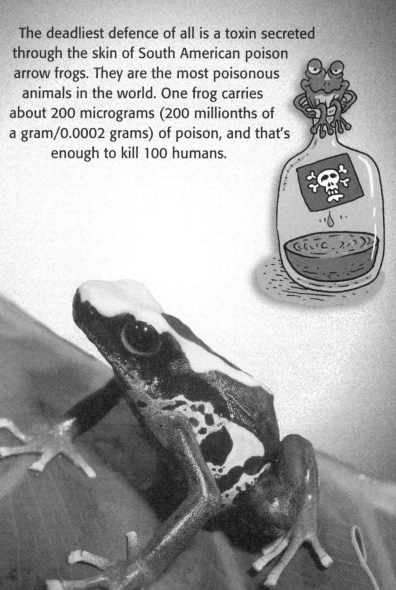

# 3
# GETTING TOGETHER

Mating rituals in the animal and insect world have evolved over millions of years. Males and females respond to each other in ways that are unique to their species. They all ensure the birth of new generations, so the species will live on.

## Wedding presents

Not many of us would fancy the life of a spider, but especially not a male spider. In many species the female is much larger and stronger than the male. She's always hungry and will make a meal of the male if he comes too close, or makes an abrupt movement while in her web which tells her he's there. It makes you shiver to think of it. So the male keeps out of the way most of the time.

The problem comes when he and the female want to mate. The black widow female spider, for instance, will often kill and eat the male straight after mating. (No prizes for guessing why the species has that name!) She only has to mate once. She stores the male's sperm, then fertilises her own eggs as she lays them in her sac.

In some spider species the male has devised a way of escaping the female's clutches. He brings her a present. Before approaching the female, the male catches a fly or some other food morsel – usually one bigger than himself – and wraps it up with his silken thread. He gives this to the female and then quickly gets on with the mating business while she is busy unwrapping her parcel.

By the time she has done so, the male has completed his task and scurried off to safety.

In other species the male plays tricks on the female. Either he satisfies his own hunger by sucking out the juices from his gift and wrapping up the empty husk, or he doesn't put anything in the parcel at all. By the time the female has discovered the deceit, he is long gone. Even so, it's a risky way for the male to reach freedom!

## CAGEY TACTICS

The male daddy longlegs weevil is a real jealous type. He keeps his female partner caged up during and after mating so that no other males can get near her. And he uses his own body as the cage. The male weevil's legs are so long that he towers over her and she can't get out between them. That's what I'd call real stand-over tactics!

# All tied up

Another type – the male European Crab Spider – has discovered an even safer way to have sex. He uses his own thread to spin a fine, veil-like net to bind up the female during the act of mating. By the time she has broken free, wanting to devour him, he has finished and departed.

# Headless mate

Before you begin to think that males of the insect world might be winning the battle of the sexes, check out the praying mantis. This female is a real horror. Actually both the male and females are vicious predators that will attack and kill animals much larger than themselves – like frogs and lizards, even small birds. But when it comes to mating, the male can be in big trouble – terminal trouble.

In some species, the female mantis will reach around during mating and bite the male's head right off. Scientists think that this male sacrifice actually helps reproduction by prolonging the mating process. Amazingly, the male body keeps going for an hour or more by an impulse that is not connected to his brain. After mating, the female will often devour the rest of the male's body, possibly to give her extra nourishment for the development of her eggs.

Please don't bite my head off... Please don't bite my head off...

It seems these cannibal habits begin at birth. Often the first meal of a young mantis after hatching is one or more of its brothers and sisters.

# Flashers

Fireflies, sometimes called lightning bugs, are the flashers of the insect world. They are not flies at all, but beetles, and they have the amazing ability to create a cold light called bio-luminescence. The light is created when two chemicals in their bodies combine in the presence of oxygen. The interesting thing is that the beetles flash their lights on and off in distinct patterns so that males and females can find each other to mate. Each species has a different flash pattern, and a male will not fly down to a female that sends the 'wrong' signal.

There's always a catch. The females of some species have learned how to copy the flash patterns of another species. The male of the copied species flies down eagerly, ready for action. Instead he is captured by the pretending female and eaten. That must be the ultimate con trick – obviously flashers are not always what they seem.

# Changelings

Something even weirder happens on Australia's Great Barrier Reef. Clownfish, which live among the stinging tentacles of anemones, can actually change sex.

Some species are bright orange with three white stripes edged in black. Others are pink with a single white stripe. These fish are all born male, but can change to females when they get bigger. They are usually in groups of four or five – one female, a smaller male and a few juveniles. If the dominant female dies, the male will change sex to become the dominant female, and one of the juveniles will develop into a fully adult male.

The pygmy angelfish on the Reef do the opposite. They gather as a group of females dominated by a male. When he dies, one of the females changes sex to become the male in charge of this watery harem. But it seems there's a limit. No male can cope with more than 10 females. I guess there's no such thing as Superfish! If the number goes higher, the largest female turns into a male, makes off with some of the remaining females and sets up his own headquarters somewhere further along the reef.

## Sex-mad

Although there are no Superfish, there is a small Australian mouse-like creature called an antechinus that could go for the title of Supermarsupial. In the mating season, which lasts about two weeks during spring, the male of the species goes sex-mad. He will spend up to 12 hours at a time continuously mating with a female before going to another – as many as possible during the mating period. He doesn't eat or sleep, he just has sex. Biologists think the long matings with each female make it more likely that the male's sperm will be successful.

The male antechinus's antics eventually wear him out. He gets thin and bedraggled, his hair falls out and he's likely to become diseased. By the end of the two weeks he's starving and so exhausted that he doesn't live long afterwards. But it does mean that young males have no competition from older adults during the next breeding season. The title of 'Supermarsupial' certainly isn't a long-lasting award. In the end the females are left to bring up the next generation on their own.

What happens in other animal families? Turn to the next chapter where you'll find that some parents take great care of their young. Others are not so gentle, and in a few species the children kill to be born.

# 4

# FAMILY BUSINESS

Over time, animal species have developed their own
special ways to give their offspring the best chance of
survival, so that the healthiest young ones grow up to
produce the next generation. This keeps the species
alive. It's not always gentle care. Parents may
kill some offspring so the others can
live, and there are some species
where the mother dies
so the children can
survive.

# Piggyback

Maybe you've heard about a story that has a 'sting in the tail'. Well, it might have been said with a scorpion in mind. There are more than 800 species around the world. Most of them have a stinging tail, and about 50 have poison that is deadly to humans.

Even the babies have an effective sting, although for the first two weeks of life they ride around on their mother's back and let her protect them. She seems to be very tolerant, even stopping to let one crawl up again if it falls off. At least, she does when times are good. If she hasn't found any food for a while and gets really hungry, the mother will start to eat her babies. Think about that when you're mucking about in the back seat of the car and Mum is driving.

# Gruesome birth

In some spider species, the young are not hatched from eggs. Instead they develop inside the mother and eat their way out of her abdomen, killing her in the process.

This also happens with a tiny insect called a mite, except the process is even more bizarre. The young mites hatch in their mother's womb, and the one male that is produced then mates with all his sisters, still inside the mother. After that, all the young mites need to feed, so they eat the mother's body tissues, then cut holes in her body to reach the outside world. The young male dies soon afterwards, but the females move away to begin the process again.

Scientists say that all the reproduction is done within the mother's body because this provides protection for the one male and ensures that he is able to find and mate with his sisters and give the brood the best chance of survival.

# Killers in the nursery

Even stranger goings-on occur inside a grey nurse shark. For a start, the female shark has two wombs, and each contains egg cases. The young sharks develop in the eggs, feeding off the yolk. When all the yolk is eaten, they hatch from the egg cases, inside the mother. The first ones hatched eat all the unhatched eggs and then hunt down and kill each other until only two baby sharks are left – one in each womb. Usually the survivors are the ones that hatch from the eggs first, because they have a start on the others.

The brothers and sisters inside the mother are an important source of food for the surviving sharks. These two survivors need to grow big enough (about a metre long) to be able to hunt and swim away from danger as soon as they are born.

Mum! He's looking at me funny again!

The mother's two wombs mean there is double the chance a young shark will live to continue the species.

## Busy mum

Australia's kangaroo takes the prize for most devoted parent. A female kangaroo can be minding three young ones at a time – a joey about nine months old that follows her around; a young joey still in the pouch; and an embryo in her womb. To cope with her joeys' different needs she even produces two types of milk. One is high in fat for the older joey that pokes its head into the pouch to drink. The other is a protein-rich drink for the joey still in the pouch.

A joey is born after only five weeks gestation in the mother's womb. It is blind, deaf and hairless, and not much bigger than a $1 coin, yet it makes its way through the fur on mother's abdomen to the pouch. There it clamps onto a teat to feed.

In the meantime the mother mates again and has another embryo in her womb. Amazingly, she can halt its development until the other joey leaves the pouch (or dies for some reason). When that happens, the new embryo will begin growing at once. She can also halt development of the embryo in times of drought. This is a way of controlling the kangaroo population so the existing animals have enough to eat.

# Tuned in

Your friends would think it pretty strange if you went into a supermarket and began talking to the cardboard containers in the egg section. They'd say you were cracked yourself. Well, maybe it's not so odd, because a mother mallard duck talks to her eggs. And the eggs talk back!

The mallard begins the conversation about two weeks after the eggs have been laid. That way the embryos inside the shells begin to learn the sound of their own species. Even more importantly, they learn to recognise the mother's voice. The eggs also make sounds. Experts think they are communicating with the other eggs in the nest so that they all hatch at the same time.

As soon as the ducklings have hatched, they gather round the mother and respond to her calls to follow. The family doesn't hang around. Mother and ducklings move out of the nest and abandon any eggs that have not hatched with the others. It's bad news for any egg that's deaf.

In other species, like chickens, the eggs make sounds which the mother hen seems to recognise as calls to sit on and warm them, or get off for a while because they are becoming too hot. But eggs also obey Mum's orders. When she makes an alarm call because a predator like a snake or fox is near, they all go silent.

# HOT STUFF

Can you call all girls 'hot' and guys 'cool'
(or the other way round) and never be wrong?
Some reptiles can.

For a number of reptile species, like alligators,
crocodiles and turtles, the sex of the babies depends
on the temperature of the eggs.

• Alligator eggs kept in a nest that is less than
30 degrees Celsius will hatch into females only. If
the nest temperature is more than 34 degrees, the
hatchlings will all be male.

• For Australian freshwater crocodiles, there's a good
chance females will hatch in a nest temperature kept
at constant temperature. But there will *definitely* be
all females if the temperature is 31 degrees or less,
or 33 degrees and higher. Males will hatch only if the
nest stays between 31 degrees and 33 degrees.

• For sea turtles, females are born in warmer
nests – about 32 degrees. Temperatures of
around 28 degrees will produce all males. If the
nest temperature is midway between (around
30 degrees) an equal number of males
and females will hatch.

# Male mothering

In some species it's the male that looks after the young.
Take the emu. After the female has laid her eggs
(up to 15 in a nest), the male moves in and sits on
them till they hatch. That takes between 58 and 61 days
and often he won't move off the nest the whole time.
The female emu will sometimes stay and defend the
nesting territory during incubation time. But often she
will move right away and pair up with other males and
lay more eggs, each time leaving the male to keep the
nests warm.

The males will also look after the chicks when they
hatch, guarding them from predators such as eagles,
snakes and goannas, for 18 months
until they are fully grown.

In seahorse families the male
has an even more specialised job.
He is the one that gets pregnant. True!

The female's only task is to deposit her
eggs into a pouch on the male's abdomen.
She then leaves him to do the rest.

Sea you later!

Sometimes more than one female deposits eggs with a male. His pouch swells up with the load.

The male fertilises the eggs, which then become attached to the pouch wall and they are nourished until hatching time. When the eggs hatch, the larvae (which are tiny replicas of their parents) remain in the pouch, fed by fluids, for about seven weeks. Then the male seahorse wraps its tail round a strand of seaweed for support and ejects the young into the water. There can be as many as 14 000 miniature seahorses in the pouch, and the birth takes nearly two whole days.

## House-hunting

Finding a place to make a nest or bring up the young has led to some very unusual house arrangements in the animal kingdom. Take the black jewel beetle.

It's also known as 'the firebug' because this little insect is always looking for a hot spot. When it senses a bushfire it won't head away from the flames, but towards them. It can detect a fire from several kilometres away. It's looking for a charred tree in which to lay its eggs. Sometimes the wood is still smoking and much too hot for humans to touch. For the jewel beetle this is ideal, because there are no enemies near and no competition.

Then there are those, like the cuckoo, that don't even try to build nests of their own. This bird will simply lay its egg in the nest of another bird species, leaving 'foster' parents the job of bringing up the chick.

Every species has its cheats, but some cliff swallows are particularly anti-social. They will lay their eggs in the nest of another cliff swallow in the same colony. They sometimes throw out an egg that's already in the nest. Birdwatchers have even seen these swallows carrying an egg in their beaks and dropping it into a neighbour's nest as they fly past.

Scientists think some birds use other birds' nests because it saves them from the task of feeding and rearing their chicks themselves. It leaves them stronger and free to use their energy to produce more eggs. By placing one egg in each of a lot of different nests, they also reduce the chance of predators killing all their offspring. Maybe that's where we got the saying 'Don't put all your eggs in one basket.'

Not every animal stays in the same territory. In the next chapter there are stories of animals that are amazing travellers – always on the move, always going places.

# 5

# GOING PLACES

Many animals are nomadic. Whenever food or water becomes scarce in one place, nomads move on to another where it is more plentiful. Other animals are migratory. They often travel huge distances when the seasons change, to escape bitter cold winters, searing hot summers or drenching monsoon rains. Their journeys can be across whole oceans and continents.

# Flying Snakes

Imagine you are walking through a grove of coconut palms somewhere in Singapore and something whizzing through the air catches your eye. It's not a bird. It's not a plane . . . and it's not Superman either because it's too thin and doesn't have a red cape and blue bodysuit.

It's likely to be a Paradise Tree Snake. Okay, this reptile doesn't actually fly, but it is one of several snake species that can spring out of one tree and glide across to another. Gliding lets them get to another tree without going all the way down the trunk and back up the next one. They can also catch prey in the air or escape predators quickly.

The amazing thing is that these snakes don't have flaps of skin like a glider possum to help them stay airborne.

Instead the snake flattens out its ribs and creates a U-shaped hollow along the underside of its body, the way you do when you suck in your stomach. This hollow groove catches a cushion of air that slows the reptile's fall, like a parachute. And, just as a parachutist pulls on ropes to change the direction of flight, the snake twists its body in mid-air to control its path.

The snakes have been known to 'fly' for 100 metres, but the distance depends a bit on the height of the launch tree. If the next tree is too far, they don't mind crash-landing on the ground. They aren't hurt, and the ridged scales on their bellies make it easy to grip tree trunks and climb up high again. It seems they've invented a new game called Snakes without Ladders.

# Rocket launchers

Biologists say that the world high-jump record is held by the common flea. The best of them reach a height of 20 centimetres. That's huge for such a tiny insect. It's like an Olympic high-jumper leaping an eight-storey building.

Fleas feed on blood from animals like rats, squirrels, cats, dogs and humans. They don't have wings, so they use their leaping power to quickly board their restaurant as it passes.

Even more amazing, fleas don't actually jump. They are launched like a rocket and accelerate at 50 times the speed of the American space shuttles. This power is generated by two elastic pads on the insect's knees. When the flea kneels ready for flight, the pads are compressed, like the spring of a jack-in-the-box when the box is shut. The insect locks itself into this crouched position with two hooks attached to its legs. Then it releases the hooks and the elastic pads spring back into position, propelling the flea in a head-over-heels flight to land feet first, grabbing at its target.

They never get tired, either. Scientists have recorded fleas taking off thousands of times without stopping. No Olympian could ever compete with that.

# Aquanauts

It's very hard for humans to compete in the water too, especially against seals and penguins. Penguins can swim at speeds up to 25 kilometres per hour and almost continuously for three to five months of each year. Over that time they travel about 1500 kilometres. That's the same as spending two whole school semesters (and the holiday in between) swimming from Melbourne to Sydney and back without stopping.

Seals are even more impressive. The male northern elephant seal, for instance, spends half the year at sea and travels 21 000 kilometres between Mexico and Alaska. But it's in the diving department that these seals are really amazing. They regularly go down to 800 metres and the deepest dives are more than 1500 metres (1½ kilometres) below the sea surface, holding their breath for up to two hours at a time.

Seals don't get the 'bends' either, like human divers. These are hideously painful (even fatal) cramps that divers get when they come up too quickly after being in the high pressure of water at the ocean depths.

To prevent this, humans must stop every now and then on the way up to let their bodies gradually get used to the lower pressures at the surface.

Seals have a much better system. They actually breathe out, not in, before they dive. Then they collapse their lungs on the way down. This forces the remaining air into special airways that don't connect with the animal's bloodstream. That means seals can rise to the surface as quickly as they like without any air bubbles forming in their blood. The seal conserves oxygen during its dive by slowing its heartbeat to about a tenth of its normal rate, and directing most of its blood to its heart and brain.

# POLE TO POLE

When it comes to long-distance travelling,
no creature can rival a little bird called the Arctic
tern. The adults are about 35 centimetres long,
with a wingspan of just 80 centimetres, and
weigh only 120 grams. Each northern winter they
fly from the Arctic islands down to the Antarctic to
catch the southern summer. It's still freezing cold,
but the days are long and there's plenty of food.

When winter comes to Antarctica the terns fly all
the way north again. These birds make a round
trip of 35 000 kilometres every year. Arctic terns
usually live for 30 years, so that means each bird
will travel more than a million kilometres in its
lifetime. Think how many frequent flyer points
the family could get for that.

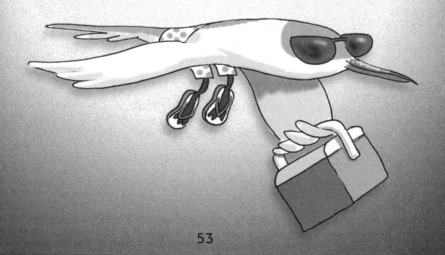

# A long flitter

The migration of the Monarch
Butterfly is even more astounding.
It's not as far as the terns
– about 3000 kilometres from
Canada down to California and
Mexico and then back again.
But for a frail insect,
that's a very long flitter.
Millions and millions of
these orange-and-black butterflies fly about 60 metres
above the ground in a steady stream each year, away
from Canada in winter and then back again to breed
during the spring. The monarchs only live for nine
months, so they don't make the trip more than once.
Yet their children and their children's children return
to the same places every year.

Many of the places where they land are big tourist
attractions in America. Some reports say that you can't
see the bark on the trees for butterflies, and that the
branches sag under their weight.

Are we
there yet?

In every group there are butterflies that don't follow the usual crowd. Wanderers have somehow made their way across the Pacific Ocean to south-eastern Australia, and their offspring now migrate from Melbourne to Sydney or Adelaide each winter to avoid the cold.

## Fishy overlanders

Australian short-finned and long-finned eels are long-distance travellers too, and they can move over dry land as well as in the water. The young eel larvae are spawned in the Coral Sea between Queensland and the Pacific islands, at depths of 300 metres or more. Slowly, by the action of currents, they are brought back to the Australian coast into river mouths, where they develop into small versions of their parents. Then they leave the salt water and migrate upstream into fresh water to develop into adults. Some get as far as Victoria to live in ponds and lakes.

The salt content of fluids in a young ocean eel's body is in balance with the salt water around it. When it swims into rivers, fresh water seeps in through the eel's skin (by a process called osmosis) to dilute the salt in its body fluids until balance is restored between the amount of salt in the water inside and outside its body. Excess body water is expelled as urine so the eel doesn't become waterlogged.

The eels do not fully mature until they are 20–30 years old. These adults then return to their birthplace in the sea to spawn. Those starting from isolated billabongs, ponds or lakes have the most difficult journey, because they have to get out of the water for part of the way to find a river system. They do have a slimy body, which makes it easier. They can wriggle like a snake across moist grass, which helps to keep their skin from drying out during the overland bits.

When they swim out into the sea, osmosis works in reverse. The eels lose water from their body through their skin and drink salt water to avoid dehydration. The excess salt is expelled in urine.

The eels' journey back to their birthplace in the Coral Sea can be as long as 4000 kilometres. They make the journey only once. After spawning, they die.

The Asian Clarias Catfish is another that can live

out of water for a long time. It has a second breathing organ to get oxygen directly from the air, and often it will 'walk' from one pond or river to the next. It is a big fish, over half a metre in length, and it wriggles and jumps along by twisting and turning its body. Mostly this happens at night and in the rain – then its skin stays moist and isn't exposed to the sun.

It just goes to show that a fish out of water is not always helpless. Maybe we should believe a fisherman who talks about the one that walked away. That's a good lead-in to the next chapter, which is about animals that are pretty smart.

# 6
# SMART AS

Humans are not the only intelligent creatures on Earth. There are a number of wild animals that are very clever at making and using tools, finding their own medicines, mimicking other species and learning from experience.

## Tooled up

You've probably seen chimpanzees in a circus or on TV that have learned all sorts of tricks, like riding bicycles, putting on clothes, counting out items into separate piles and even using sign language. Chimps are obviously very clever, and they don't need humans around to teach them, either. In the wild they often make tools out of the materials around them.

They will crush leaves and grass to make a sponge so that they can soak up water for drinking, or brush some sticky substance from their hair. They will also strip away the bark of carefully chosen twigs and poke them into a termite or ant nest and pull out a tasty snack of insects – well, they're tasty to a chimp anyway. Sometimes they'll use a heavy stick to break open hard-shelled nuts, or as a weapon to wave threateningly at predators or rivals.

Sea otters are tool-users too. They have learned that stones can be used to crack open juicy shellfish like clams and mussels. The otter floats on its back, holding the shellfish in its front paws, with a heavy, flat stone on its stomach. It pounds away on the stone until the shell cracks open. An otter will hang onto a good stone while diving for the next course.

# Bird-brains

Other tool-users are
even more surprising.
There's the Goliath
Palm Cockatoo,
for instance, a large,
black-feathered bird
with bright red patches

on its face that lives in New Guinea and on Cape York
Peninsula in Queensland. It's like a drummer in a bush
band. During courtship, a male cockatoo grasps a stick
in one foot and beats it on a hollow log to attract mates
and warn rivals. This makes a booming sound that is
heard kilometres away. The males also call for their
mates, with open beaks. Biologists say the bird's red
cheeks go even redder when it's excited – not surprising
when it acts like a rock 'n' roll star.

There's another bird in Australia that could be the
band's vocalist. It's a species of shrike, better known as
a butcherbird, and it has one of the most melodious
songs of any bird. It even sings duets with its mate.

Why is it called a butcherbird? Well, these birds will impale their prey of grasshoppers and other insects on the spikes of a thorn bush, often while the insect is still alive. The spike is a handy place to hold and store the bird's meal – like a butcher hanging meat.

In Africa, Egyptian vultures have a different mealtime problem to solve – getting through the wrapping. If you have a delicious but tough-shelled ostrich egg, how do you break it open? Simple – throw rocks at it. Vultures can pick up stones weighing about 500 grams (half a kilogram) in their beaks and throw them half a metre with a flick of the neck. Their aim is good, and it takes about eight direct hits to crack the egg.

Other birds use more delicate ways to gather a meal. On the Galapagos Islands there's a finch that snaps off a cactus spine and holds it in its beak to pry for insects under the bark of trees. Crows living further west, across the Pacific on New Caledonia, go one better. They use their beaks as scissors to make hooks and sharp spikes from twigs which they use to pull out grubs living in tree branches.

They also cut jagged edges from palm fronds which they use as rakes when foraging for insects among earth and fallen leaves on the ground.

## NUTCRACKER

The smartest crows must be the ones in Japan and some parts of the USA that have learned to use human technology. They will put walnuts on the road so that passing cars run over them and break them open. It beats trying to use their beaks as nutcrackers.

# What's up, Doc?

Some animals have learned the skills of doctoring. Many will take medicines they find in the bush when they don't feel well. Chimpanzees are a good example. They have been seen picking the leaves of a plant called Aspilia, which is a member of the sunflower group. The chimps squash the leaves in their hands and then pop them in their mouths for 10 seconds or so before swallowing. It must taste bitter, because the chimps pull faces and give other signs that they don't enjoy it.

Researchers have found out that the Aspilia plant contains a special oil that kills parasitic worms and bacteria found in the chimps' stomachs. Somehow the animals know that taking this medicine will make them feel better.

## Diet Supplements

There's a famous place called the Kitum Caves in Kenya, Africa, that herds of elephants regularly visit. Heavy rainfall in the area leaches mineral salts – like

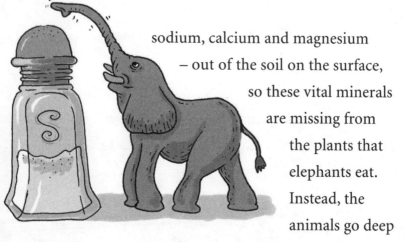

sodium, calcium and magnesium – out of the soil on the surface, so these vital minerals are missing from the plants that elephants eat. Instead, the animals go deep into the cave system, where the minerals have been washed down from the leached zone above. They use their tusks to gouge out chunks of wall which they then chew and swallow.

The mountain gorillas of Rwanda, Africa have special places in the forest where they scoop out and eat fistfuls of earth rich in minerals. In the Amazon region of South America there are places where colourful birds called macaws nibble at exposed banks of mineral clays.

Biologists think that for all these animals and birds the salts and the clay help to settle their stomachs, counteracting toxins (natural poisons) found in some of the plants and seeds that they eat.

The red deer on the Shetland island of Rhum in Scotland have a much more gruesome way to get the calcium they need. They bite off the heads and legs of shearwater chicks and crunch up the bones. In this way they make their own bones and antlers strong.

# Anting

If you've ever been camping in the bush, you'll know that pitching a tent over an ants' nest isn't much fun. It's even worse if you accidentally stand on a nest, especially if they're bull ants. But there are a number of bird species which do exactly that on purpose. Believe it or not, it helps the birds to keep their feathers clean and free from fungi, bacteria and parasites.

When ants are stirred up or threatened, they squirt out defensive substances that sting and smell. The birds want to spread these strong substances through their plumage, right down to the quill ends. They will often sit directly over a nest and fluff up their feathers to let the ants run all over them, squirting the fluids as they go. At other times the birds will pick up one or two ants in their beaks and stroke them through their outstretched feathers to make sure the ant 'lotion' is rubbed right in. It's a bit like putting antiseptic on the skin. It probably stings a bit – but at least the birds can snack on the ants afterwards.

# Farming

Although ants come off second-best to birds in the anting process, they do all right when it comes to farming. Often they herd and protect other insects, like aphids and mealy bugs. These tiny insects suck the sap from plants, and produce sugary globules of honeydew. Ants just love this honeydew, so when they find a large group of feeding aphids or mealy bugs, ants will first 'milk' them for the honey and then protect them while they produce more.

Sometimes the ants will build a shelter of leaves to shield and fence in the aphids during the day. They

have even been known to herd their honey-producers
back to the ant colony at night and then take them
to a new spot to 'graze' the next day, just like a farmer
with a herd of milking cows.

## Perfect crime

The octopus has the best eyesight of any animal.
People have reported an octopus pulling the cork out
of a bottle to get at a small fish or crab inside. It has
even been known to sneak out of its tank at night, slide
over and into the next tank and eat the crabs there.
Next morning, the aquarium staff see a tank with
no crabs, and the octopus back in its own tank with
nothing to show it has carried out the midnight raid.

## Mimic

Remember the 'Supermarsupial'
in Chapter 3? Well, there's an
Indonesian octopus species
called 'Wonderpus' because it is an amazing mimic.

It can quickly change its shape to look like a sea snake one moment (by anchoring seven of its arms down a hole and waving the other about in the water), a lionfish the next and maybe a sole (fish) soon afterwards.

Researchers think Wonderpus uses this mimic act for two reasons. It may change to look like the poisonous lionfish or sea snake to deter predators, or it might mimic the harmless sea star (starfish) to lull its own prey into a false sense of security so that the prey comes close enough to catch.

Then there's the cuttlefish, which belongs to the same class of animals as the octopus, but is even sneakier. It fools its own kind.

During mating the cuttlefish males form into groups and cluster around a female, but it is the dominant male – the biggest and most colourful

– that gets to mate most often. Sometimes the biggest males are so intent on fighting off rivals that the female is left unguarded for a few moments. Here's where a sneaky one comes in. He's even called a 'sneaker male'. Usually he's smaller and hasn't much of a chance of breaking through the ring by force.

While the other males are trying to look fierce and impress each other by rippling colours down their bodies and waving their eight long arms hung with banner-like flaps, the sneaker sees an opening to the unguarded female and he darts in and mates with her.

At other times the sneaker male will pull his arms in and produce mottled colours on his back to make him look like a female and lure the big males towards him. Suddenly he will dart back through the pack and mate with the real female before the rivals realise what's happened.

That's enough brainpower for the moment. Next chapter slows things right down and looks at animals that take time out for several months of the year.

# 7

# TIME OUT

In countries with very hot summers or really cold
winters, when it is unbearable to be outside and food is
scarce, some animals survive by going into a controlled
'sleep' that may last for months. A few could even be
described as the living dead.

## Desert survivor

When the rivers begin to dry up during the harsh
summer of southern Africa, the African lungfish
burrows its way into the mud of a stream bed and
seals itself into an envelope of mucus that enables
the creature to stay moist during the long drought.

It keeps a tiny hole open to the surface of the ground and (this is very unusual for a fish) it can breathe oxygen directly from the air, using its swim bladder as a lung.

The water-holding frog in Australia also buries itself in the sand and fills its outer skin with moisture so it looks as if there's a plastic sack around the animal. This enables the frog to stay moist and alive until the rains come. The eggs of freshwater shrimps, small fish and insects can also survive the harsh desert conditions for years. Then they quickly hatch in the puddles and lakes formed when it finally rains.

## The big chill

In Alaska and Canada, several types of frogs, like wood frogs and chorus frogs, have the opposite problem – how to survive the icy winter. Well, they actually freeze almost solid. More than two-thirds of the water in their bodies turns to ice and their hearts stop. Cut these animals and they won't bleed, yet they're still very much alive.

In most other animals, including humans, freezing temperatures causes ice crystals to form and burst through blood-vessel walls. Skin and blood cells are also damaged by freezing (we call it frostbite). Polar explorers and mountaineers often lose fingers and toes because of this problem. For the wood and chorus frogs, it's a different story.

When ice begins to form on the frogs' bodies, their livers begin to produce extra glucose, which is a blood sugar. This substance acts like anti-freeze, flowing into the body cells to protect them from damage. At the same time, water in the cells drains out into the spaces between them. This water freezes, but does no damage to the body organs.

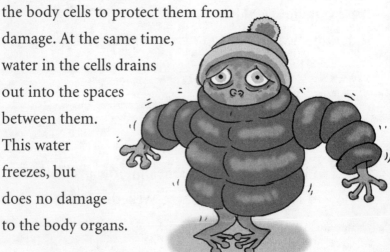

There are also a number of bugs, like the Arctic Woolly Bear Caterpillar, that can survive frozen solid with no ill effects for 10 months in the tundra, where temperatures plunge to minus 50 degrees Celsius. The Arctic Ground Squirrel allows its body to cool below freezing too, 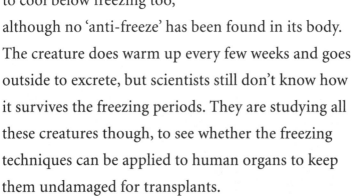 although no 'anti-freeze' has been found in its body. The creature does warm up every few weeks and goes outside to excrete, but scientists still don't know how it survives the freezing periods. They are studying all these creatures though, to see whether the freezing techniques can be applied to human organs to keep them undamaged for transplants.

## Feathered Snoozer

While many birds migrate to get away from cold winters, there is one bird in parts of North America that stays put. The poorwill, a member of the nightjar family, is the only bird known to hibernate. Nobody knew this until 1946, when a poorwill was found, apparently dead, in a rock crevice in winter. Its body was cold, there didn't seem to be a heartbeat, and there was no response to light shone in its eyes. But after a bit of prodding, it stretched a wing. The bird was alive and well.

Researchers have since found that this bird can lower its body temperature by about 17 degrees Celsius. This is remarkable, because a drop of only 3–4 degrees in body temperature is enough to kill a human. People have even found hibernating poorwills under a cover of snow.

The birds can remain in this controlled sleep for many weeks, awakening in warmer weather with no ill effects.

# RECHARGING
# THE HUM

The tiny hummingbird conserves its energy
by going into a deep, deep sleep (called torpor)
every night. Its heart rate drops, its breathing
slows down and its body temperature falls.
It only uses one-twentieth of the energy needed
for normal sleep. The bird sleeps so deeply that
it takes 20 minutes to be fully awake in the
morning. Are you like that? You can always
tell Mum you are recharging your
batteries for a busy day.

Hibernation doesn't sound much fun – like staying
in bed the whole of winter. I'd prefer to spend 'time out'
during cold winter days in front of a warm fire with
a good book. In the next few pages you'll find some
unusual facts about animals that you can use to impress
your mates and teachers, or maybe surprise your family
at the next fireside gathering.

# 8

# ANIMAL CRACKERS

There are some facts about animals that don't fit into any category. They're just weird. Try these.

Octopus, cuttlefish and squid have three hearts. This helps to maintain blood pressure to the ends of their long arms. Two of the hearts are extras on either side of the body and they pump blood to the main central heart.

Flounder begin life as a normal fish and swim upright. But then, after a few weeks, one eye migrates either across its head or through its head, depending on the species, to be right next to the other as the adult fish turns over to swim on its side.

Hi Flounder—
you look flat
out as
usual

The South American Anableps fish appears to have four eyes. It swims on the surface with the waterline at the centre of each eye so it can watch above water for predators and underwater for prey at the same time.

✳ Sea stars (the new name for starfish) push their stomachs out of their mouths to envelop and digest their prey from the inside out. When finished they pull their stomachs back into their bodies.

✳ Rabbits, hares and some other rodents eat their own faeces because they don't get all the nutrients out of their food the first time around.

✳ The monkey-like Golden Gentle Lemur of Madagascar happily eats and digests the young shoots of giant bamboo. This plant contains cyanide. Each day the lemur eats 12 times the amount of cyanide poison needed to kill a human.

✳ The feathers of flamingo can be a range of colours from pink to deep red. But the colour is not natural. It comes from the food these birds eat. They prefer algae and tiny organisms which contain red pigments.

✳ Some species of swiftlet, a cave-dwelling bird in tropical Asia, make their nests entirely of their own spit. This gluey saliva sets into a solid, rubbery material which is prized as an ingredient for the Chinese delicacy called birds'-nest soup.

✳ There's a small bird called a fairy tern living on tropical islands in the Pacific and Indian Oceans that doesn't bother to build a nest at all. Instead the female balances her single egg on a bare branch or a palm frond away from other birds and predators. Incubation requires a great deal of skill and caution, especially when it comes time to change over for the male's turn to keep the egg warm.

✳ The glass frog has transparent skin on its belly which makes it possible to see the frog's intestines, its beating heart and its circulating blood.

✳ Snapping turtles have large heads and strong jaws and include dead animals in their diet. They can quickly detect dead and rotting flesh, and police have used them to help search for human corpses lodged underwater.

✳ Koalas have pawprints so much like human fingerprints that it is nearly impossible to tell them apart. Maybe police should be looking out for 'Killer Koala' at a crime scene!

✳ Tigers would be easily detected, though, even if they were shaved bare. They have stripes on their skin as well as through their fur.

✳ Tree-dwelling sloths in the rainforests of Central and South America spend their lives hanging upside down. Moss-like algae grow on a sloth's fur in this humid atmosphere, adding a greenish tinge that helps the animal blend in to the leaves and branches.

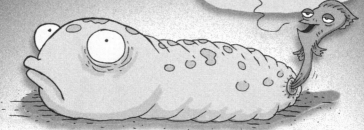

Oh, I hope you don't mind – I invited my friend the whale to come and stay....

# WEIRD TENANT

The prize for the weirdest back-door tenant must go to a thin little fish called a pearlfish. It actually lives in the anus of some sea cucumber species like the Beachball Sea Cucumber, which is a large, slug-like creature related to sea stars.

The sea cucumber doesn't have gills. Instead it breathes by drawing in water through its anus and absorbing oxygen internally from that water. The little Pearlfish has made use of this water movement by wriggling into the anus tail-first and taking up residence. It doesn't seem to pay rent either, because there is nothing that the sea cucumber gains from this squatter. Even worse than that, the pearlfish often nibbles away at its landlord's internal tissues – a bit like a human house-guest breaking up the furniture for firewood.

✳ A female giraffe stands up to give birth. The newborn calf falls more than 2 metres to the ground. The jolt helps it to take a first breath and clear its breathing tubes.

And if thinking about that doesn't give you a headache, pity the poor woodpecker.

✳ High-speed film shows that a woodpecker's beak strikes a tree about 20 times a second. The reason the bird doesn't knock itself out is that the skull is specially reinforced. A pillow of cartilage between the beak and the skull acts as a shock-absorber. There's also a bit of space between the brain and the skull so the brain doesn't bounce around inside the woodpecker's head and become scrambled.

The animals you've just read about may seem strange or gruesome, but they are all well equipped to survive and reproduce. They have developed a size and shape, or colour, or body temperature, or digestive system, or a way of reacting to other animals and plants that works in their particular environment. This is called animal adaptation. What about humans? Perhaps we are the odd ones. What other species has to use a knife and fork because its teeth aren't sharp? Or wear clothes to keep warm because it doesn't have fur? Or switch on the light so it can see at night? And what other animal has to stay with its parents for more than 10 or 15 years before it can survive on its own? That's us. To the rest of the animal world, we might seem really weird!

RICK WILKINSON began searching out and writing stories when he was about ten, so he could never be found when his parents wanted him to mow the lawn. He liked reading about animals and wanted to be a zoologist when he grew up. But he became a geologist instead, and learned about amazing fossil animals like mammoths, sabre-tooth tigers and dinosaurs.

He discovered that fossil animals buried deep in the earth make oil, so he changed jobs to become a journalist and write about the explorers who look for oil and natural gas in jungles, deserts and deep oceans. He writes animal stories in his spare time and still tries to get out of doing household chores.

MIC LOOBY is an illustrator and writer who lists his hobbies as chewing pens and humming softly.

84

# Thanks

Thanks to Josephine Denis and Jason Caruso at the Melbourne Aquarium.

Thanks also to Patrick Honan (head of the invertebrate department), Chris Banks (co-ordinating South-east Asian conservation programs) and Jenny Hoysted (education centre) at the Royal Melbourne Zoological Gardens; and to Matt Vincent, acting head of Healesville Sanctuary, Victoria.

*Rick Wilkinson*

The publishers would like to thank Professor Gisela Kaplan for checking the draft text. Thanks to BrandX Pictures and photographer Burke Triolo for two pictures from the Bugs & Insects collection (pages 24 and 29), and Ruth Grüner for the photo on page 39. Thanks also to istockphoto.com and the photographers named for images appearing on the following pages: page vi Dane Wirtzfeld; page vii Suzannah Skelton; page 14 George Ihring; page 21 Kevin Tate; page 25 Terry McGleish; page 26 Paul Topp; page 35 Emily May Walden; page 43 Heather Cash; page 47 David Higbee; page 63 Jan Abt; page 67 Peter Chen; page 75 Rob Sylvan; page 76 Elisabeth Cölfen (calamari), Brian Eggertsen (stethoscope); page 78 J. Spencer; page 82 Stephanie Asher; page 83 Matthew Hull.

# Glossary

**abdomen** an animal's belly, or the middle part of an insect

**bio-luminescence** a kind of light made by living things

**colony** a collection of animals of the same kind living together

**conserve** to use something a little bit at a time to make it last longer

**dehydration** the loss of water from an animal's body

**dilute** add water to make a weaker mixture

**disgorge** bring food that has already been swallowed back up through the mouth, usually to feed young

**dominant** most senior or most powerful

**embryo** a baby animal in its mother's womb, or in an egg before it is hatched

**fertilise** combine with (an egg)

**foraging** searching for food

**gestation** the period of time before birth when a baby (embryo) is in its mother's womb

**hibernate** stay asleep or inactive, usually without food or drink, during winter

**incubation** the time before eggs hatch when they are kept warm by the parents sitting on them or by the sun's rays

**irritant** something that itches or stings or makes an animal feel uncomfortable or unwell

**larvae** the baby form of insects, frogs, seahorses (often nothing like the grown-up animals)

**juvenile** young or baby animal

**membrane** the moist, soft tissue that covers and protects the organs in an animal's body

**mesmerise** hypnotise

**migratory** animals (particularly birds) that travel long distances to escape cold winters, hot summers or heavy rains

**mimic** a 'copycat' animal that copies the sounds or behaviour of an animal of a different species

**nomadic** animals that move from place to place, looking for food and water

**nutrients** minerals and vitamins in an animal's food that keep it alive and healthy

**parasitic** living in, on or with an animal of another species and getting food from

**plumage** a bird's feathers

**predator** an animal that hunts and kills other animals to eat

**spawn** lay eggs (fish or frog)

**toxin** a poison that occurs in Nature, not a man-made one

# Where to find out more

## Books

John Farndon, *4000 Things You Should Know About Animals*, Miles Kelly Publishing, Great Bardfield, Essex, 2002

Seymour Simon, *Animals Nobody Loves*, SeaStar Books, New York, 2001

Bruce Thomson, *Australia's Most Deadly and Dangerous Beasts*, Lothian Books, Melbourne, 2004

*World Book's Animals of the World* (a series by World Book Inc., Chicago)

*Nature Watch* (a series by Lorenz Books, London)

## Websites

*Australia's zoos and aquariums have good websites:*

- www.zoo.org.au (Zoo Victoria)
- www.melbourneaquarium.com.au
- www.zoo.nsw.gov.au (Sydney Zoo)
- www.perthzoo.wa.gov.au
- www.adelaidezoo.com.au
- www.almaparkzoo.com.au (Brisbane Zoo)

*Some websites with lots of information on animals:*

- www.worldwildlife.org
- www.yptenc.org.uk/docs/animal_facts.html
- wildwnc.org/af/index.html
- www.kidsplanet.org
- www.worldalmanacforkids.com/explore/animals.html
- www.zooish.com
- www.yakscorner.com/index/animals.html

*Some websites featuring weird animal behaviours:*

- www.bbc.co.uk/nature/animals/reallywild/amazing
- wcs.org/7490/kidsgowild/
- www.yahooligans.yahoo.com/content/animals
- oceanlink.island.net/oinfo/hagfish/hagfishathome.html
- www.enviroliteracy.org

## For teachers

Charlotte Uhlenbroek, *Talking With Animals*, Hodder & Stoughton, London, 2002

Tim Flannery & Peter Schouten, *Astonishing Animals*, Text Publishing, Melbourne, 2004

# Index